GRANDPA

Sea Shells

`Published in 2013 by
Speechmark Publishing Ltd, Sunningdale House, Caldecotte Lake Business Park,
Milton Keynes, MK7 8LF, UK
Tel: +44 (0) 1908 277177   Fax: +44 (0) 1908 278297
www.speechmark.net

Text Copyright © Jo Johnson 2013
Illustrations Copyright © Lauren Densham 2013

002-5931/Printed in the United Kingdom by Hobbs
British Library Cataloguing in Publication Data
A catalogue record for this book is available from the British Library

ISBN 978 0 86388 997 4

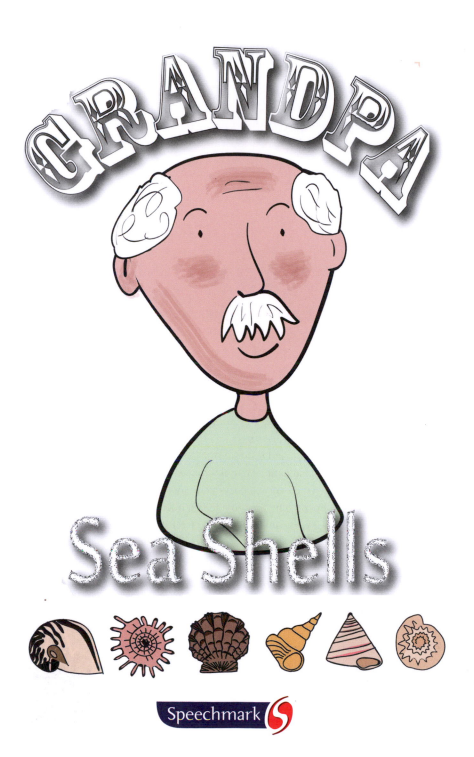

NOTES FOR PARENTS

'Grandpa Sea Shells' tells the story of three young children who spend a day with their grandparents after their grandfather has been diagnosed with dementia. The book is intended to support conversation at the time of first changes in a relative, a diagnosis of dementia and mild to moderate progression. Families and clinicians have told us this is the time period when they need material to support their explanations to children. Whilst the book could be used to start a conversation about any form of dementia, most of the key symptoms described in this story reflect the typical features associated with the Alzheimer's type, as this continues to be the most common.

This book has been designed so that children of between four and ten can read it independently. Ideally it should be used with an adult to facilitate discussion about all aspects of family life and to enhance general emotional wellbeing. The book deliberately makes dementia one of many things going on for this family and highlights things that families can still enjoy together. We have included ideas for positive activities at the end of the book as well as puzzle and description pages that children can enjoy doing with a family member, teacher or clinician.

Families often ask, "How can we talk to children about dementia?" The answer is straightforward: you can talk to them about dementia in the same way that you talk to them about all other aspects of your lives as a family. Honesty is vital; children always know if things are being kept from them and consequently imagine things to be much worse. They need to know that dementia is not something that can be caught or made worse by their behaviour.

Children need to be given information that is relevant to the specific type of dementia that has been diagnosed in their family and be told that symptoms will get worse as time goes on. For the Alzheimer's type that would probably include forgetting, having trouble with words, frustration, anxiety and reduced tolerance to noise. Whilst some children might enjoy a little information about the parts of the brain that are changed, most children just want to know how it will impact them: Can grandpa still go swimming and kick a football? Will mum be able to take them to ballet or do the cooking? As the dementia progresses, this information will need updating.

Children need an opportunity to ask questions and to feel that it is all right to talk about any changes in their relative which they are finding puzzling or upsetting. As their understanding improves they will need more information.

The story is intended to emphasise that all families are unique with their own strengths and weaknesses and different experiences. Dementia is another experience that some people encounter and others do not.

Given that dementia is a set of symptoms rather than a single condition, every family will be different in terms of symptoms and progression. Use the book as a template to enable you to create your own book that is personal to your family life. Together, create a book that includes the names and adventures of your family and the positive and negative experiences that dementia creates.

Jo Johnson

Consultant Neuropsychologist

v

The concept of a sea shell house is based on the true story of beach warden, Ted Sutton from Camber Sands, East Sussex. If you follow the link www.britishpathe.com and type "sea shells artist (1958)" into the search facility, children can see him collecting shells and decorating his house in a three minute BBC documentary produced in 1958.

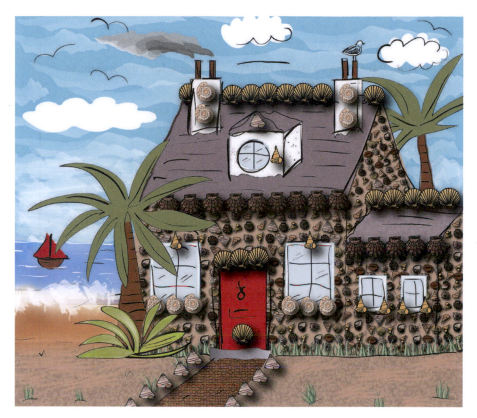

Today is my grandpa's birthday and we are going to see him.

He lives in a little cottage near to the sea with Gran. I call him 'Grandpa Sea Shells,' because when Grandpa was as young as dad is now, he covered all the walls of his house with sea shells.

It looks beautiful even though some of the shells are old and broken now.

'Children!' shouts Grandpa when we get to the gate. Grandpa usually forgets our names, but he is always VERY happy to see us and he always has a peppermint in his pocket for me. Yum yum.

My name is Leah and my brothers are called Oscar and Theo. They are twins. Gran always remembers our names.

'Happy Birthday, Grandpa!' says Oscar. 'You are 70 today.'

'Am I?' says Grandpa. 'That is very old!'

Gran laughs. 'No it's not,' she says. 'You can still run faster than me!'

3

Gran gives us some of her homemade lemonade.

'Lovely yellow,' says Grandpa.

He sometimes can't think of the right word. Sometimes I can't think of the right word when I do writing at school.

I don't like writing.

Reading is better.

Gran brings in a big chocolate cake with lots of candles. 'Mmm,' says Grandpa, 'I smell cake!'

Grandpa starts the singing. 'Happy Birthday to you! Happy Birthday to you! Happy Birthday dear Grandpa, Happy Birthday to you!'

We all join in and I blow out the candles.

 I dip my finger in the chocolate on the cake when no one is looking. Yum yum!

Oscar throws a ball at Grandpa and he catches it and smiles.

Grandpa likes kicking the ball with Oscar and Theo. The boys love playing football with Grandpa because he lets them cheat and throw the ball!

Dad says you are only allowed to kick it.

'Let's go to the beach!' says Gran.

Mum puts some sandwiches, drink and crisps in a bag, while the boys play ball and I eat chocolate. Mmm!

'Quick,' says Gran, 'Shut the door or Dougal will fly away!'

Grandpa shuts the door, says, 'Goodbye birdie bird,' and laughs.

Dougal is Grandpa's canary. He flies around the house and sits on his head when he is eating yummy things like cake. Dougal always makes Grandpa smile.

We love Dougal too.

On the way to the sea Grandpa carries the bag.

I hold Grandpa's hand. It feels warm and wrinkly.

I skip all the way to the sea and Grandpa laughs a lot.
Everyone feels happy.

Oscar and Theo run into the sea and splash Gran and Mum.

I sit with Grandpa on the stones. We don't like getting wet.

Grandpa rolls a stone at me and we play marbles. I love playing with my grandpa. He has good ideas for games.

Mum, Gran and Oscar run out of the sea and Gran
unpacks the ham sandwiches.

'Where is my cheese?!' Grandpa shouts, 'I want my
cheese!'

Gran looks sad.

I don't like it when Grandpa shouts.

Oscar gives Grandpa some crisps and we all eat cake
and forget about cheese. Yum, yum!

'Come on,' says Gran, 'Grandpa and I need a sleep. Let's go home now.'

Grandpa holds my hand and we sing "Skip to the loo my darling."

Gran laughs and says, 'you are singing the wrong words - it should be "Skip to my Lou, my darling"!'

Everyone laughs and sings our words as we skip back to the house.

time one return home

Grandpa loves singing.

He used to sing in a choir but now he just sings with me.

Gran falls asleep in her favourite chair and Mum goes to do the washing up.

I finish off the cake. Mmm, it's yummy!

'Can we look at the photos?' shouts Theo.

Theo sits on Grandpa's lap and we all look at the photos of Grandpa when he built the sea shell walls. Grandpa shows us a picture of dad skipping.

The boys think this is very funny.

Boys are so silly.

'It is time to go home,' says Mum.

Gran waves goodbye.

Grandpa walks to our car. He wipes the mirrors with a cloth; he always does that for Mum.

I give Grandpa a big hug.

He smiles and says, 'Bye bye Kate.' He always calls me Kate. That's my mum's name.

after That

'Mum,' says Oscar on the way home, 'Why does Grandpa forget things and get words muddled up?'

'He has dementia' says Mum.

'What's "the Mentia?"' says Oscar.

Mum laughs.

'It's called "dementia". Some parts of Grandpa's brain have stopped working properly and it makes him forget things and lose words.'

'Is that why he went the wrong way at the beach and shouted at Gran to get cheese?' Oscar says.

'You think you are so clever!' Theo says to Oscar. Mum gets cross with Theo for being mean to his brother.

'Remember when you felt frustrated that you could not build your Lego? That is how Grandpa feels when he gets muddled and can't do the things he wants to. It makes him feel sad and cross,' Mum explains.

'Dementia makes me sad and cross,' says Oscar.

'I know,' says Mum. 'It is sad that Grandpa can't do all the things he used to. It is sad for us and for Gran.'

Mum smiles and says, 'But don't forget Grandpa is still the best singer.'

'And he has big muscles!' says Theo.

'And he lets us cheat in football!' says Oscar.

'And he gives us peppermints!' everybody says at the same time.

'Yum yum!'

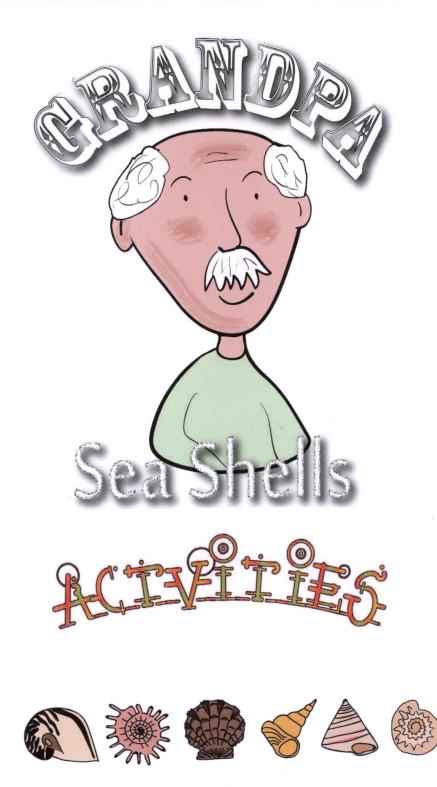

GRANDPA

Sea Shells

ACTIVITIES

ACTIVITIES

ALL ABOUT ME

MY NAME IS

Draw your favourite food on this plate

THESE ARE THE PEOPLE IN MY FAMILY

WHAT IS YOUR FAVOURITE COLOUR?

COLOUR IN YOUR EYES

I DON'T LIKE

DRAW YOUR HOUSE

I ABSOLUTELY LOVE

ACTIVITIES WORDSEARCH

Can you find the words listed at the bottom in the grid below?

n	p	s	s	x	f	i	o	y	i	i	q	o	e	u
e	k	k	i	p	a	v	k	v	i	o	p	e	o	l
q	d	m	s	n	e	u	w	n	f	g	a	o	s	k
n	y	n	e	c	g	e	o	s	u	g	d	z	m	a
t	r	i	s	b	o	i	c	y	j	k	s	n	o	i
e	o	a	w	t	s	n	n	h	l	n	i	q	t	t
g	m	r	a	u	v	y	d	g	o	i	a	e	p	n
r	e	b	f	a	t	i	k	i	r	d	g	u	m	e
o	m	n	y	e	q	n	t	t	r	a	s	y	m
f	o	i	i	y	s	o	e	j	o	i	n	r	s	e
c	t	x	q	d	m	s	o	f	h	o	o	m	a	d
i	n	q	r	e	p	b	y	e	r	e	g	n	u	d
a	x	o	z	u	y	s	j	u	f	j	l	b	v	c
r	w	i	x	s	a	t	e	p	i	r	u	p	a	o
s	j	x	a	c	u	n	i	a	y	q	c	c	p	d

upset · symptoms · forget
confusion · neurons · speech
condition · anxiety · memory
emotions · singing · words
dementia · · brain

ACTIVITIES

ALL ABOUT MY RELATIVE

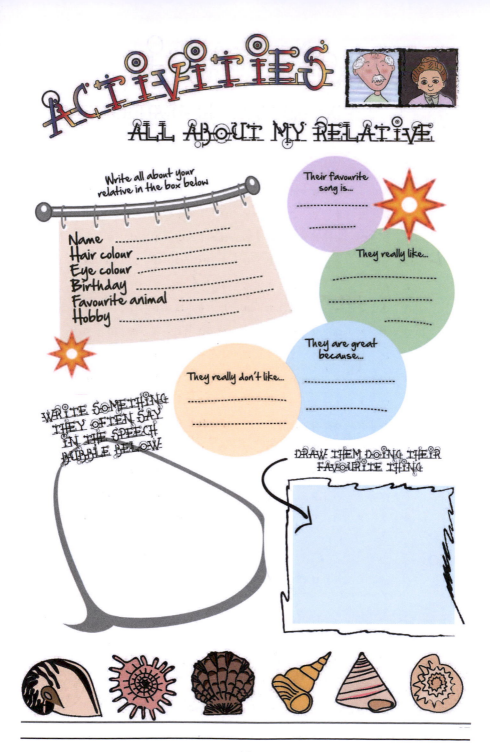

Write all about your relative in the box below

Name ....
Hair colour ....
Eye colour ....
Birthday ....
Favourite animal ....
Hobby ....

Their favourite song is...
....
....

They really like...
....
....
....

They are great because...
....
....

They really don't like...
....
....

WRITE SOMETHING THEY OFTEN SAY IN THE SPEECH BUBBLE BELOW

DRAW THEM DOING THEIR FAVOURITE THING

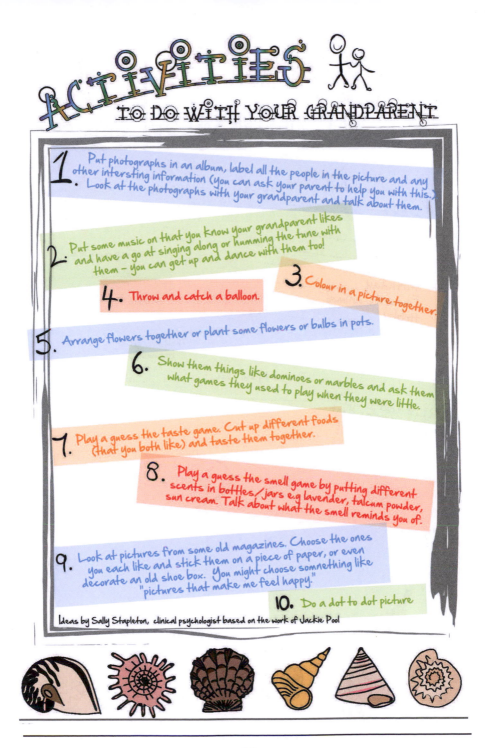

ACTIVITIES
TO DO WITH YOUR GRANDPARENT

1. Put photographs in an album, label all the people in the picture and any other intersting information (you can ask your parent to help you with this.) Look at the photographs with your grandparent and talk about them.

2. Put some music on that you know your grandparent likes and have a go at singing along or humming the tune with them – you can get up and dance with them too!

3. Colour in a picture together.

4. Throw and catch a balloon.

5. Arrange flowers together or plant some flowers or bulbs in pots.

6. Show them things like dominoes or marbles and ask them what games they used to play when they were little.

7. Play a guess the taste game. Cut up different foods (that you both like) and taste them together.

8. Play a guess the smell game by putting different scents in bottles/jars e.g lavender, talcum powder, sun cream. Talk about what the smell reminds you of.

9. Look at pictures from some old magazines. Choose the ones you each like and stick them on a piece of paper, or even decorate an old shoe box. You might choose somnething like "pictures that make me feel happy."

10. Do a dot to dot picture

Ideas by Sally Stapleton, clinical psychologist based on the work of Jackie Pool

For further information and support on dementia, please visit the websites below:

www.alzheimers.org.uk

'This is me tool' available on Alzheimers Society website. A tool for people with dementia to inform people of their interests and preferences.

www.dementiauk.org

Jackie Pool Associates

www.jackiepoolassociates.org